PREHISTORIC!

EXPLORING 4 BILLION YEARS OF LIFE ON EARTH

FOR OUR FRIENDS, JONNIE AND LESLEY WILD

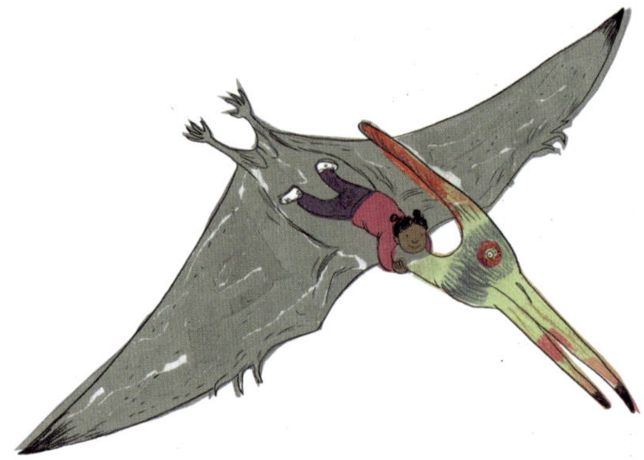

MICK MANNING and BRITA GRANSTRÖM have pioneered their unique approach to picture book non-fiction since 1993. Their awards include: the Smarties Silver Award, five English Association Awards, five Royal Society Junior Science Book prizes and two ALMA nominations. In 2020 they won the SLA/Hachette award for Outstanding Contribution to Information Books.
Their other books for Otter-Barry Books include *Books! Books! Books! Explore inside the Greatest Library on Earth and Women Who Led the Way: Great Explorers and Adventurers.*

The authors and publisher would like to thank Peter Riley for his expert advice as science consultant for this book.

Peter Riley was head of Moorhead High School science department before becoming an international, award-winning author of science books for primary and secondary school students.

First published in Great Britain in 2019 and in the USA in 2020 by Otter-Barry Books Ltd, Little Orchard, Burley Gate, Herefordshire HR1 3QS.

This paperback edition first published in Great Britain in 2024 by Otter-Barry Books

www.otterbarrybooks.com

ISBN 978-1-915659-40-8

Illustrated with watercolour, crayon and montage

www.mickandbrita.con

Printed in China

1 3 5 7 9 8 6 4 2

MIX
Paper | Supporting responsible forestry
FSC® C104723

PREHISTORIC!

EXPLORING 4 BILLION YEARS OF LIFE ON EARTH

MICK MANNING AND
BRITA GRANSTRÖM

Otter-Barry BOOKS

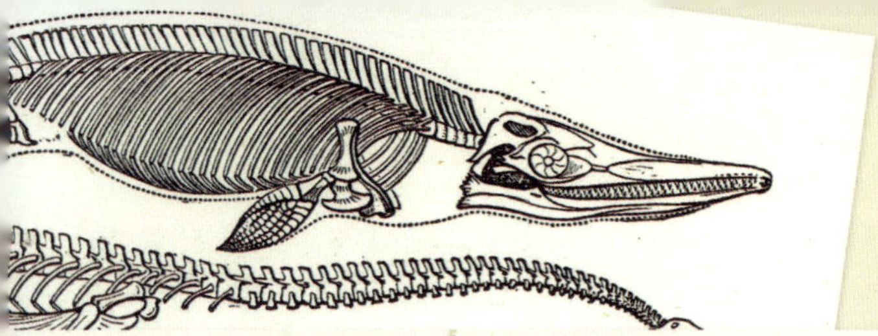

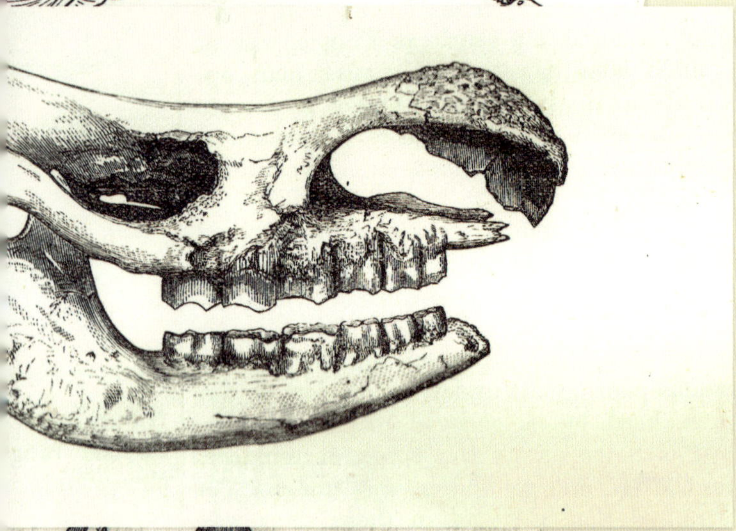

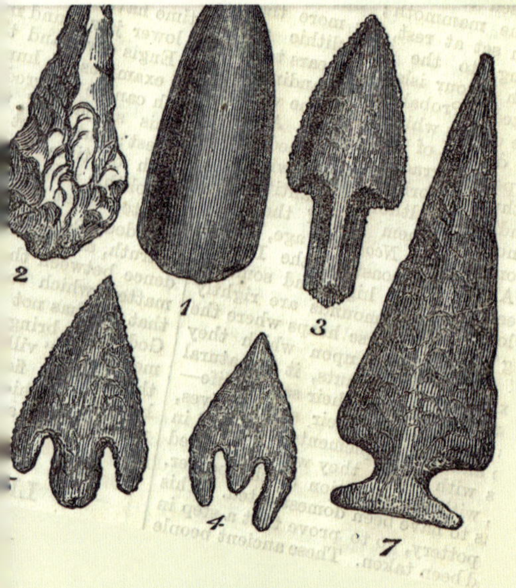

CONTENTS

Our facts are bang up-to-date and checked by experts!

The History of Prehistory is our story of what happened on planet Earth, long before anyone knew how to write anything down. Travel with us and witness the history of prehistory happening before your eyes, from Earth's fiery beginnings to the explosion of life on our planet and beyond. Based on all the latest scientific discoveries and research, in this unique journey through 4 billion years you can 'live' prehistory by flying with a pterosaur, hanging out with apes, riding a mammoth and lots more.... Are you ready to go?

Volcanic Planet

Hadean Eon, 4.6 to 4 billion years ago

Look! Monstrous volcanoes spew out lava (molten rock) and asteroids (massive lumps of rock from outer space) crash-land and explode, smashing Earth's surface to pieces. Life can't begin yet, the planet is choked with stinky, poisonous gases, but as Earth slowly begins to cool down it gives off steam, steam that turns to rainwater....

One huge asteroid smashed chunks off our planet. The chunks went into space-orbit around Earth, eventually clumping together to become our Moon.

WOW!

Volcanoes are caused by the pressure of magma forcing its way to the surface from deep in the Earth's crust.

Life Begins

Archean Eon to end of Proterozoic Eon, 4 to 2.5 billion years ago

For millions of years all that water has remained lifeless due to Earth's poisonous atmosphere. But now, as super-heated water, rich in minerals, bubbles out of deep underwater cracks in Earth's crust, the very first living things, called ***Archaea***, have come into being. Over time, nourished by this rich chemical soup and thriving in the warm mineral-rich water from the vents, they will develop into many different sorts. Eventually, one type, blue-green algae, moves nearer the surface and makes its own 'food', using a process called **Photosynthesis**.

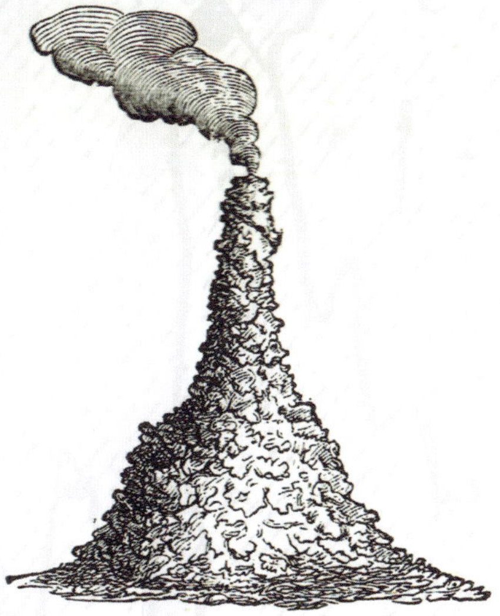

Super-heated by the magma under the Earth's crust, water bubbles out of hydrothermal vents, and the minerals it contains build up to form chimneys known as 'smokers'.

By about 2.4 billion years ago photosynthesis has enriched the air with life-giving oxygen.

Photosynthesis

In photosynthesis sunlight energy is used to transform water and carbon dioxide gas into a sort of sugar – food energy. The process uses up poisonous carbon dioxide and releases life-giving oxygen into the water and the air as a by-product. Photosynthesis made it possible for other living things to form.

Life Explodes

Cambrian Period, 541 to 485 million years ago

As carbon dioxide levels drop and oxygen goes up, life in the silent underwater world is changing. Here, more than 480 million years in the past, we can see an 'explosion' of new life-forms. Some have developed new body parts to help them burrow, paddle or swim. Some have grown the first-ever eyes! There are sea worms and snails, giant shrimps and enormous shellfish; there are trilobites, jellyfish, sponges and corals.... Over time, the first backboned fish will begin to develop.

Fossil of a Trilobite. There were over 20,000 different sorts of Trilobite and they roamed Earth's oceans for about 270 million years.

Life Moves onto Land

Late Silurian Period, 420 million years ago

Plant life has spread from the water to the land. Mosses, liverworts and hornworts grow close to the ground, but the plant ***Cooksonia*** is different. It reaches up a little above the surface and has tubes inside it to take up water from the ground. As these plants die and rot down, they form the soil in which other plants begin to grow. Above these plants grow weird giant fungi called ***Prototaxites***.

Mosses first appeared on land almost 400 million years ago.

Those red ones are Cooksonia, one of the oldest known land plants...
These Prototaxites aren't trees, they're giant fungi! Whatever next?

Fish Fingers

Late Devonian Period, 375 million years ago

These big creatures are a sort of fish called ***Tiktaalik*** and they have specially adapted fins that act like fingers – these 'fish fingers' help them to crawl about this muddy beach. They live their lives half-way between land and water. So long as they stay wet they can even 'breathe' air through their skin.

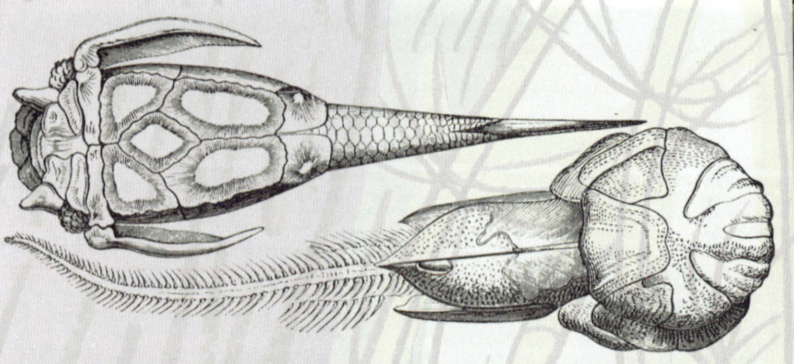

Fossil remains of two small armour-plated fish that lived during the Devonian period.

Tiktaalik are a distant ancestor to all modern-day land animals with backbones....
These guys can grow to about 3 metres long – 10 feet!

Swampy Waters

Late Carboniferous Period, 299 million years ago

About seventy million years later, in these deep, swampy waters, monstrous, scaled fish such as ***Rhizodont*** prowl. Trees can now stand tall, using tough woody trunks and deep underground roots to anchor and balance them. These dark forests grow thick, covering huge areas of the planet, and are home to countless new insects, amphibians and reptiles.

Layers of dead trees and plants fossilised over time to become coal. Meanwhile the shells and skeletons of sea creatures were forming limestone.

I wonder if we'll see a Rhizodont? It's the largest freshwater fish that ever lived.
I hope it doesn't see us first! I don't want to be fish-food!

Swamp-Forest Adventures

It's been a breathtaking adventure so far; it's taken hundreds of millions of years from the Cambrian to the end of the Carboniferous – and that's a mind-boggling amount of time. Let's take a break and tell you a bit more about some of the things we found out....

275 million years ago, ***Eryops*** was one of the first large animals to live on land. It was an amphibian, like modern-day frogs and toads, so it had to return to the water to lay its eggs.

Sun and wind were very important in helping reptiles and amphibians to warm up or cool down.

Over time, some amphibians evolved to become reptiles, who laid their eggs on land. To be entirely land-based was a huge advantage, and reptiles like ***Dimetrodon*** dominated the Earth for millions of years, until gradually a new sort of reptile evolved – dinosaurs!

Many invertebrates – animals without backbones such as worms, snails and insects – colonised the land. ***Meganeura*** were giant dragonflies – the adults were the size of a modern-day seagull.

Diplocaulus was a stocky amphibian with a large boomerang-shaped head. It could grow to about a metre (3 feet) long. They were a favourite food of fierce Dimetrodon.

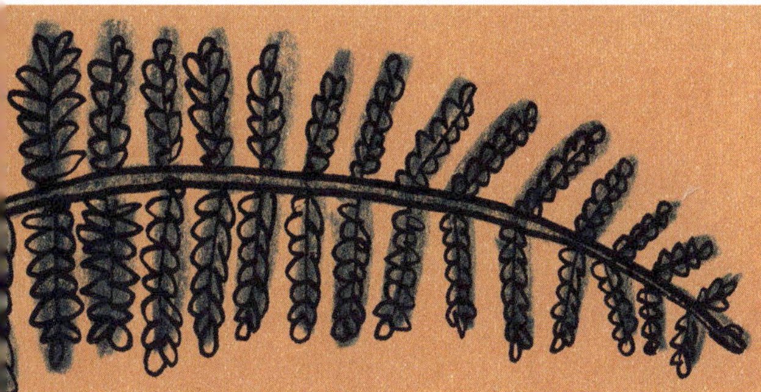

Ferns were one of the most common plants of the Devonian and Carboniferous periods.

Wattieza were one of the earliest trees. Standing up to 8 metres (26 feet) tall, with fern-like leaves, they could push above competitors to reach the sunlight.

There are many different sorts of pterosaurs, and they're not dinosaurs, but flying reptiles...

Terrifying Pterosaurs

Jurassic Period, 200 to 145 million years ago

Hold on tight, this is the craziest fairground ride you can imagine! As the golden age of the dinosaurs stretches before us, look out below as we pass over a herd of long-necked Diplodocuses browsing on tall trees. We're cruising through the sky on the backs of two mighty pterosaurs. Flying reptiles like this rule the skies for about **150 million years!**

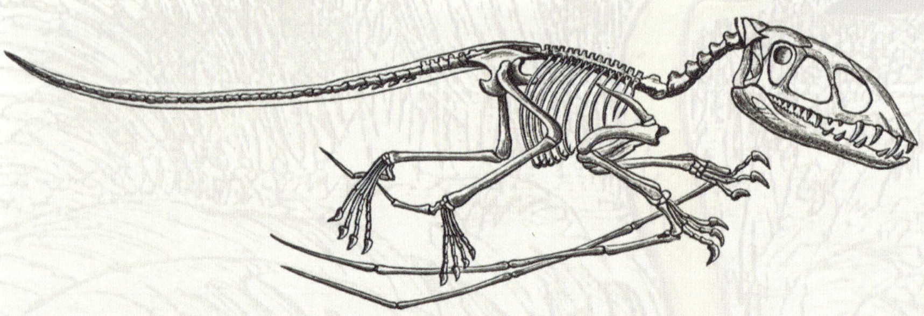

This is the skeleton of a smaller pterosaur called Dimorphodon. Like many pterosaurs it had large holes in its skull to reduce the weight of its huge beak. The wings were supported by long finger bones.

...and they aren't the ancestors of birds either – we're going to meet them next....

Feathered Dinosaurs

Cretaceous Period,
145 to 65 million years ago

With their feathers and bird-like walk, dinosaurs such as this Velociraptor really are the ancestors of modern-day birds. This one is hungry and she's hunting one of our early, furry ancestors. Different types of tiny, shrew-size mammals began developing in the Triassic Period but by now some are bigger. Alphadon grows to the size of a small squirrel, and is probably very tasty if you happen to be a raptor – so ***Shhhh!***

Many of the first small, furry mammals like Alphadon hunt at dusk for insects, seeds and perhaps even dinosaur eggs.

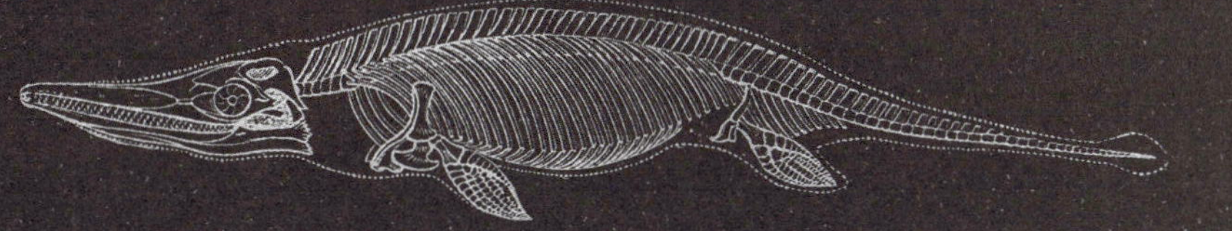

Giant fossils found in sea cliffs, such as this Ichthyosaur, show that huge sea reptiles roamed the seas while dinosaurs ruled the land.

When Dinosaurs Ruled

Triassic Period, 251 - 200 mya

This period began after Earth's most severe known extinction event, probably caused by a huge asteroid colliding with Earth. About 96% of all sea creatures and 70% of land animals were wiped out, and it took about 10 million years for the planet to recover. When it did, reptiles ruled, both in the seas and on the land. The stage was set for the age of the dinosaurs.

Sea reptiles such as **Plesiosaurs** hunted the seas from the beginning of the Triassic until the end of the Cretaceous Period.

Cynognathus was a 'dog-like reptile'. It may have had fur and given birth to live young instead of laying eggs.

Archaeopteryx was one of the first flying 'bird dinosaurs' and it had a beak.

The length of **Brachiosaurus** has been estimated at 26 metres (85 feet) That's as long as two buses or a railway carriage....

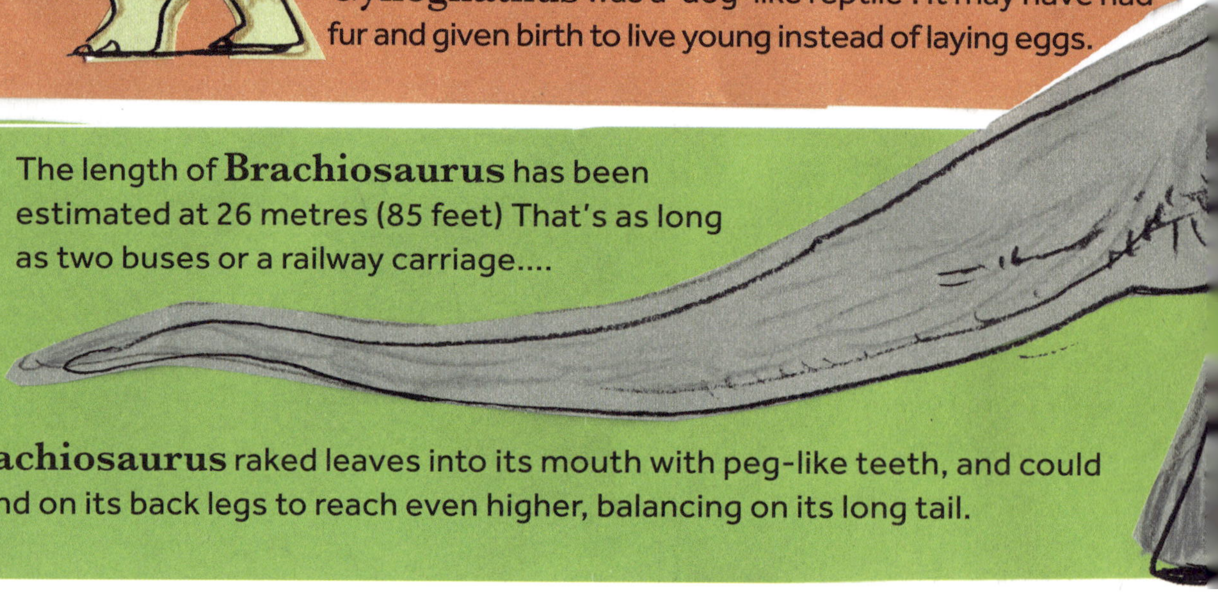

Brachiosaurus raked leaves into its mouth with peg-like teeth, and could stand on its back legs to reach even higher, balancing on its long tail.

Cretaceous Period, 145 - 65 mya

Although dinosaurs still ruled the earth and feathered birds developed, it was also the period when non-flying dinosaurs, sea reptiles and pterosaurs became extinct.

Triceratops was a 7 metre (23 feet) long vegetarian built like a tank. It had thick skin and huge horns for protection from predators, but also, perhaps, for courtship-display fights, like modern-day reindeer and buffalo.

About 66 million years ago yet another massive asteroid collided with Earth. Three quarters of all species vanished including all the dinosaurs, apart from birds.

Jurassic Period, 199 - 145 mya

By this time Earth was dominated by dinosaurs, from huge herbivores such as Brachiosaurus, reaching into the treetops, to many fierce carnivores like the mighty Allosaurus. There were also the flying reptiles, the first birds and the first furry shrew-like creatures: our earliest mammal ancestors....

Pterosaurs were flying reptiles. Some were small, others could grow very big; some fed on fish while others scavenged, rather as modern-day vultures do.

Allosaurus (left) was about 8 metres (26 feet) in length and at the top of the food chain, preying on large herbivores.

T. Rex had the strongest bite of any animal that ever lived – yet probably lived mostly by scavenging already dead dinosaurs. Its chicks may have kept warm with a sort of downy fluff, like giant ducklings.

Velociraptor (left) was a 2 metre (7 feet) long carnivore that may have hunted in packs. Its large claws were as sharp as knives and its feathered arms probably helped it to balance when running and leaping on large prey.

Life in the Treetops

Late Paleocene Period, 66 to 56 million years ago

It's now well over five million years since the asteroid explosion wiped out the dinosaurs. Mammals dominate the Earth, and some of them are huge! We've been playing with a giant sloth bear whose head reaches into the treetops! I'm sitting with a ***Plesiadapis*** troop. They live in the tree tops for safety, but forage the grassy plains for roots, small lizards and insects. They will become the ancestors of monkeys and apes.

This is the skull of an ancient predator, the large Arctocyon, also known as a 'bear-dog'. Like modern bears, it was large and could climb trees when hunting.

Swinging in the Trees

Miocene Epoch, 23 to 5 million years ago

We're swinging through the trees with these agile apes. Our playmates may be the far-distant relatives of both us humans and of chimpanzees. They are monkey-clever, with grasping hands and the power to think things through; they communicate too, making noises and pulling faces as they swing above the forest floor. One day, still far in the future, their descendants will become the **great apes**, venturing out of the trees and able to walk on two legs.

Toumai's species is *Sahelanthropus tchadensis*. It could grip with hands and feet much like those of modern chimpanzees (1 and 2).

Lucy's Family

Pliocene Epoch, 5.3 to 2.6 million years ago

We're in Africa, meeting one of our earliest two-legged human ancestors, ***Australopithecus afarensis*** – scientists have named her Lucy. She lives in a family group, who hunt for insects, seeds, roots and even meat scraps such as these prey remains left by a sabre-toothed cat. A family group has lots of eyes and ears to spot food or danger. They shout loudly to scare away predators, and pass on information with ape-like gestures and grunts – it's not language as we know it, but it is the start of something.

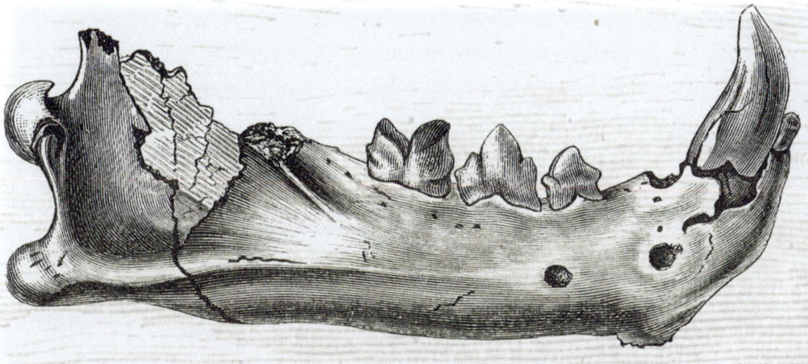

This is the jawbone of another prehistoric big cat – a cave lion. Lucy's skeleton, discovered in Ethiopia, has a carnivore's toothmark on its hip bone; but scientists are unsure if that's how she died – she may have fallen out of a tree.

From Ape to Human

It took millions of years for us to swing out of the trees and slowly become human. Here are just some of the key stages in our development....

It's been a long journey from back then to right now! Grasping hands, walking upright, using tools and fire... the power to think things through and eventually to talk, made us what we are today....

Sahelanthropus tchadensis

7.5 - 5.6 million years ago

Our earliest ape-like ancestors parted from the gorillas about 8 million years ago and later with chimpanzees, sometime between 7.5 million and 5.6 million years ago. Over millions of years they slowly evolved, changing their habitat, diet and body-shapes and gradually adapting to walking upright.

Australopithecus afarensis

3.5 million years ago

Lucy's species stood just over a metre (3 feet 3 inches) tall and walked upright on two legs, gathering food from the grassy plains of Africa. The man who discovered her bones named her Lucy after a song by The Beatles.

Homo habilis

2.4 - 1.5 million years ago

Although very ape-like in looks, they had developed a larger brain than Lucy. They were perhaps the first human ancestor to make and use stone tools.

Homo erectus
1.9 million to about 143,000 years ago

They were fast runners who could hunt, control fire and may have invented stone-tipped spears. Over time, their descendants, known as Homo heidelbergensis, branched into two species: Neanderthals first, and later, Homo sapiens. These species spread out of Africa in various waves of migration.

Homo neanderthalensis
200,000 to about 30,000 years ago

Neanderthals were tough and good hunters but eventually became extinct as a species about 30,000 years ago. However scientific tests on Neanderthal bone samples reveal that many modern-day humans still have between 2% and 4% Neanderthal DNA! Such a high percentage after all this time proves that they didn't die out completely but interbred with humans.

Homo sapiens
200,000 years ago

'Humans' spread from Africa about 60,000 years ago, coming back into contact with Neanderthals as we did so. We co-existed in many parts of the world for thousands of years with Neanderthals and with heidelbergensis too, but perhaps human skills in problem-solving and our much longer childhood (a time to learn and grow) helped us become the most successful species.

Scientists believe we shared the planet with at least three of our relatives for thousands of years: Homo erectus, Homo heidelbergensis, Neanderthals and maybe others....

Woolly Mammoth Safari

Paleolithic Era, 2.6 million to 12,000 years ago

We're exploring the Ice Age, a time when Earth's temperatures plummeted and much of the Earth froze solid. Look at the glacier 'flowing' between the mountains: a slow but unstoppable ice giant, bulldozing valleys and crushing up rocks to leave sand and gravel in its wake. For animals, life has become a battle for survival. This baby mammoth is wrapped up in warm fur and, safe with his mum, he seems to be having great fun holding on to her tail as we all plod through the blizzard.

Mammoths are elephant-like creatures. They use their huge tusks like snowploughs to reach plant food and for defence against predators.

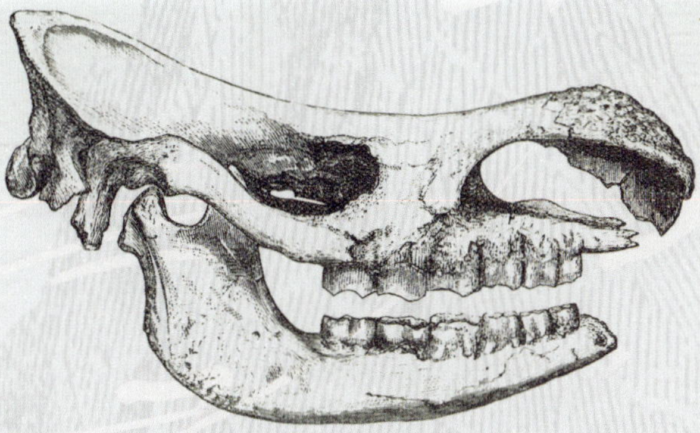

This is the skull of a woolly rhino. Just like mammoths, they grew shaggy fur to keep warm in the icy weather.

Glaciers shaped the landscape we know today.

The First Art Gallery

Late Paleolithic Era

It's now 40,000 years ago, during the deep freeze of the Ice Age, and humans are making beautiful animal paintings hidden inside dark caves. Perhaps it's a sort of magic to honour the animals they hunt for food and rely on for survival? Or a kind of ceremony to thank the spirit world that they believe controls the migrating herds of buffalo and wild horses? Here in this cave, we're helping them stencil, scratch and paint – straight onto the cave wall!

Paleolithic flint arrow and spearheads have been found in many parts of the world.

Stone-Age Diary

Here are just some of the things we got up to with a family of Stone Age hunter-gatherers.

We learned how to make a fire by twizzling a stick between our hands and pushing it hard into a hole in another bit of wood. This friction made it get so hot it set fire to little bits of dry moss.

We learned how to chip away at flints to make razor-sharp arrow heads and blades.

This is a flint I made. It took me all day to get it right!

This is one of the earliest musical instruments – a bone flute.

We accidentally woke up a cave bear and it got ***very angry!***

We learned how to use a spear thrower for more power, and used a throwing stick: a sort of boomerang.

We helped chase reindeer off a cliff.... Nothing was wasted – it was eaten or made into tools or clothes. I felt sad, but humans must survive!

Beside the fire, we carved jewellery from bones. Perhaps this migrating bird pendant is a symbol of hope for the return of spring, when life can begin again....

As far back as our ape ancestors we have made sounds and gestures to communicate, but the carving of symbols in bone suggests that language may have begun at least 100,000 years ago. Some words, common to many languages, can be traced back 15,000 years, including: ***fire, ashes, mother, old, spit*** and ***hand***.

Early Farmers

Neolithic Period, 12,000 to 4,000 years ago

Here we are in the Nile Valley, about 4,500 years ago. Technology is developing and we're helping some early farmers who are using one of the most important tools in human history... the **plough**. The first hand-ploughs only scratched the surface, but this new heavy model, pulled by oxen, digs deeper, letting in water and air. This brilliant invention is helping farmers to grow extra food which can be stored or sold – and some have begun to employ others to help them work the land. Thanks to farming, many villages are developing into towns as populations soar.

The power of ancient Egypt – its religion, its buildings, pyramids, art and statues – was only made possible by farmers feeding a huge workforce: artists, architects, clerks, doctors, potters, smiths, stone-carvers and of course builders, labourers, soldiers and slaves.

The Egyptian goddess Isis, with cow-horns and sun headdress.

Farming Diary

About 12,000 to 4,000 years ago

Farming probably began in fertile valleys around Mesopotamia about 12,000 years ago with crops such as barley, wheat, peas, beans, and also fruit trees. It quickly spread. We've been helping some of the earliest farmers across the world. Take a look at what we get up to...

The first wild rice was domesticated about 8,500 years ago in China.

Gradually, the idea of growing food rather than gathering it or hunting it from the wild, spread across Europe and Asia.

Querns, invented about 8,000 years ago, meant grains could be ground into flour and bread could be made. Grain attracted rats which is why cats were domesticated...

Domestication of animals:

Dogs - 15,000 years ago.
Pigs - 11,000 years ago.
Sheep - 11,000 years ago.
Cattle - 10,000 years ago
Chickens - 8,000 years ago.
Cats - 8,000 years ago.
Horses - 5,500 years ago.

Why waste time hunting wild creatures when we can tame them and look after them here for milk and meat?

The first metal humans used to make tools and weapons was copper, about 6,000 years ago.

Smiths made moulds to the shapes they wanted and poured in the molten copper.

Axe heads

With the need to grow crops, people moved from worshipping nature gods to gods that might help the farming year: gods of sun, earth, moon and seasons.

The Bronze Age

Much later, about 5,300 years ago, coppersmiths discovered that adding tin to the molten copper made a much harder metal, an alloy, which could be sharpened better, a great help to farmers. We call it 'bronze', and that time-period is known as the Bronze Age.

Hunter-gatherers moved with the seasons, following wild food. Farming people settled in communities – sharing the work and eating the rewards. Gradually villages grew into towns and cities. Society became different too, with rich leaders and poorer workers.

Meet the First Known Author

The Bronze Age, 5,300 to 3,200 years ago

It's now 4,260 years ago and dusk is falling in the ancient Sumerian city of Ur. This is where the first true writing has developed and this is the first-ever author to be known by name. Her name, En-hedu-anna, means 'The High Priestess, Ornament of the Sky'. 'Anna' is writing her poetic hymns to the moon goddess on clay tablets. Only important people like this can write and read: it's another sort of power. It will be centuries before ordinary people can read or write, but writing down thoughts and recording events mean that prehistory is over. So sitting next to a high priestess, on a peaceful veranda scented with lemon trees, is where our prehistoric adventures end.

From scratching words on clay and wax tablets, from dip pens to typewriters, from biros to laptops... and it all began in Sumeria at least 4,000 years ago.

GLOSSARY

Archaea - microscopic organisms, the oldest known life-forms on Earth.

Boomerang - a throwing weapon shaped so that it spins back to the thrower if it does not hit anything.

Bya - billion years ago.

DNA - the unique building blocks of life, passed on by all parents to their offspring, and directing how they develop and grow.

Eon, Era, Period, Epoch, Age - measurements (in order of length) of the mind-boggling time-span of Earth's prehistory.

Evolution - how a different species of animal or plant develops from earlier ones, often to be better suited to a new environment.

Fossil - hardened 'mineralised' remains or impressions of ancient animals or plants found in sedimentary rock layers.

Fungus - a wide range of organisms, from mould to mushrooms. They absorb nutrients directly from the ground, not by photosynthesis as plants do.

Great Apes - a group of closely related primate species named Hominids, including gorillas, chimpanzees, orangutans and humans, all sharing common ancestors.

Hydrothermal vent - a deep crack in the ocean floor from which water, superheated by the magma below, is forced upwards.

Ice Ages - periods of time when much of our planet underwent arctic conditions. There have been many ice ages; our book only visits the last one.

Magma - molten rock below the Earth's crust. When it erupts it is called lava.

Minerals - naturally occurring chemical substances such as iron, chalk, salt and potassium. Many are essential for life on Earth.

Mya - million years ago.

Predator - an animal that lives by hunting and eating other creatures.

Priestess - a female religious leader.

Quern - a pair of circular stones made so that the top one rotates or rubs to and fro on the lower one, grinding seeds and grains into a gritty flour.

Sedimentary rocks - Over time, prehistoric sediments like mud or sand or dead swampy plants were compressed by their own weight into dense layers. Under this pressure, crystal formed, cementing the granules together. Over millions of years these deposits hardened into rocks such as shale, sandstone, limestone and coal.

Spirit world - the unseen beings who were believed to control the world of humans and animals. The dancers (left) wear animal costumes to attract the spirits' attention.

Stone Age - the period of time before humans learned to use metal. It lasted about 3.4 million years.

Sumeria - a region of the ancient country of Mesopotamia (parts of modern Iraq, Iran, Syria and Turkey), the world's earliest civilisation.

Play the Timeline Game

Use this game to help you remember the journey you have just made. You need a dice and some counters to play.

Hadean Eon *4.6 - 4 bya* Stay cool! START HERE		**Archaean Eon** *4 - 2.5 bya* Good job you remembered swimsuits! →		**Cambrian Period** *541 - 485 mya* Trilobites show you the way through. ADVANCE TO 11
	**Late Devonian Period** *375 mya* Fish with fingers in the Devonian. HAVE ANOTHER TURN		**Late Silurian Period** *420 mya* Canoe hits rocks! GO BACK 3	
11	**Late Carboniferous Period** *299 mya* Chased by a Rhizodont! BACK TO START		**Jurassic Period** *200 - 145 mya* High speed thrills! Swoop forward 3 places. →	
Miocene Epoch *23 - 5 mya* Hanging around. MISS A TURN		**Late Paleocene Period** *66 - 56 mya* Make new friends! HAVE ANOTHER TURN	 ←	**Cretaceous Period** *145 - 65 mya* Hiding from a raptor. MISS A TURN
 →	**Pliocene Epoch** *5.3 - 2.6 mya* Sabre-tooth chases you! GO BACK 3		**Paleolithic Era** *2.6 million - 12,000 ya* Catch a cold in the Ice Age - get warm! BACK TO START	
YOU'VE WON THE GAME		**The Bronze Age** *5,300 - 3,200 ya* Meet Anna and throw a 2 to win!		**Neolithic Period** *12,000- 4,000 ya* Help the farmers. Throw a 4 to win! ←